He was kind, too.

One day, he met an old man.

Midas helped the man
to find his house.

"My son is a god,"
said the old man.

"He can give you
a wish."

"I love gold,"
said King Midas.

10

"I wish I could touch things and turn them to gold."

King Midas touched
his stick...

...and it turned to gold.

He touched his
palace...

...and it turned to gold.

He touched his dinner...

...and that turned to gold, too.

"How can I make
it stop?" said
King Midas.

"There is a secret river in the hills," said the god.

"Find it and wash
yourself in it."

Midas walked a very
long way.

At last, he found
the river.

And the water washed
away his golden touch.

23

PUZZLES

Puzzle 1

Can you spot the differences between these two pictures?

There are six
to find.

Which order should the pictures be in?

Puzzle 2

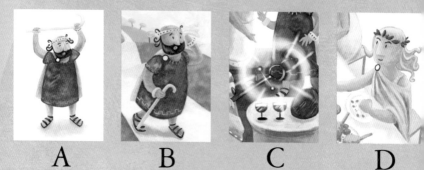

A   B   C   D

Puzzle 3

A   B   C   D

Choose the best sentence in each picture.

Puzzle 4

Puzzle 5

What happened next?

Puzzle 6

A

or

B?

Puzzle 7

A

or

B?

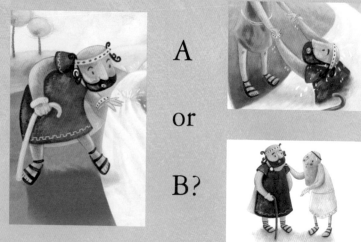

Answers to puzzles

Puzzle 1

Puzzle 2

C

A

D

B

Puzzle 3

B

C

D

A

Puzzle 4

"Hello Dad!"

Puzzle 5

"It's gold!"

Puzzle 6

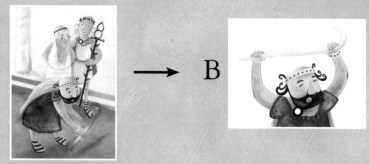

→ B

Puzzle 7

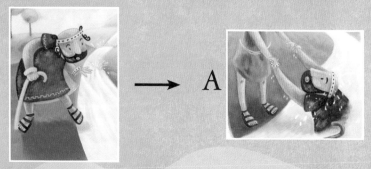

→ A

About the story

King Midas was a real king. He lived in Ancient Greece around 3,000 years ago. An old legend says he went to the river Pactolus to wash. This river is in modern day Turkey. People still say that the stones on the river bed sparkle with gold.

Designed by Caroline Spatz
Series designer: Russell Punter
Series editor: Lesley Sims
Digital manipulation: John Russell

First published in 2008 by Usborne Publishing Ltd., Usborne House,
83-85 Saffron Hill, London EC1N 8RT, England. www.usborne.com
Copyright © 2008 Usborne Publishing Ltd.